# THE BOXER

Gabriele Tinti

# The Boxer

*Translated into English by*
*David Graham & Nicholas Benson*

eris

## Note on the Edition

This book brings together poems and short prose pieces written since 2009, gathered around one of the very few bronzes to have survived from antiquity: the *Boxer at Rest.* Engaging with the sculpture itself and with the lives of ancient fighters, these texts seek to restore a sense of its mystery and enduring presence. They are shaped by a belief in poetry as a form of resistance to erasure—an insistence on endurance, a stubborn urge to persist in spite of and against everything, to contradict the end.

The sequence is structured as the script of a monologue, a kind of interior drama in which the *Boxer* and the city of Rome form the backdrop. It is not intended for the stage, but for a restrained, unspectacular reading by a single voice. Here, the *Boxer* is not a relic of the past, but a figure through which fragility, endurance, and the search for meaning within pain can be held in view.

The book is arranged in a series of movements. It opens with a section of verse presented first in Italian and then in English. Two prose poems follow, with the original and the translation set facing one another. A sequence of shorter poems comes next, again presented bilingually. The volume closes with a final section, returning to the opening structure: the poem in Italian, followed by the same text in English.

●

*All’angolo:*
*pugni a riposo,*

*ascoltando*
*antichi discorsi*

*nel tuo tempio*
*di carne e metallo*

*e sangue che*
*tamponi*

*con i guantoni*
*stringi l’emorragia*

*delle parole,*
*sfidi il destino.*

*Non c’è dolore:*
*lui ti aspetta,*

*già in piedi prova*
*con l’ombra*

*come fare*
*per meglio*

*colpire.*
*E il pubblico?*

*È in apnea*
*per quest’ultimo*

*round che non arriva*
*che non è mai*

*abbastanza.*
*Tra poco*

*dovrai alzarti:*
*apri la bocca*

*—bevi; solleva*
*la testa—guarda*

*quest'uomo*
*fatto di terra.*

*Ti basta*
*un colpo soltanto*

*tirato bene poi*
*ti abbracceranno*

*ti porteranno*
*in trionfo*

*ma il colpo*
*non viene*

*e qualcuno*
*se n'è già andato*

*nel tramonto*
*di Roma*

*in quel languore*
*che apre*

*il petto dell'arena;*
*lontano salgono*

*le urla del fianco*
*a fianco, rovina*

*di questo mondo*
*di cuori che*

*esultano*
*insultano*

*giudicano*
*e tu in tutto*

*quel rumore*
*cerchi il respiro*

*buono, il riflesso*
*nel cerchio*

*del secchio pieno*
*di sangue e saliva*

*e interiora*
*—un po' di tempo*

*ancora.*

*In the corner:*
*fists at rest,*

*listening*
*to ancient speeches*

*in your temple*
*of flesh and metal*

*and blood that*
*you staunch*

*with your gloves*
*quell the flow*

*of words,*
*defy fate.*

*There is no pain:*
*he awaits you,*

*already up he parries*
*with the shadow*

*as one does*
*to better*

*strike.*
*And the crowd?*

*Is holding its breath*
*for this last*

*round that doesn't come*
*that's never*

*enough.*
*Soon*

*you'll have to get up:*
*open your mouth*

*drink, lift*
*your head, look*

*at this man*
*of clay.*

*You need only*
*a single blow*

*well thrown, then*
*they'll hug you*

*carry you off*
*in triumph*

*but the blow*
*doesn't come*

*and some*
*have already gone*

*into the sunset*
*of Rome*

*in that languor*
*that opens*

*the breast of the arena*
*far off rise*

*the shouts*
*of the crowd,*

*collapse*
*of this world*

*of hearts that*
*exalt*

*insult*
*judge*

*and you in all*
*that noise*

*seek the deep*
*breath, the reflection*

*in the ring*
*of the tin*

*full of blood*
*and saliva*

*and bile*
*a little while*

*longer.*

*Per favore, ripeti. Non riesco a sentire quello che dici. Il mio viso è di bronzo, non lo vedi? Guarda i miei occhi, le mie orecchie, questo petto. Ripeti se vuoi. Oppure risparmia il fiato. Le parole si rassegnano davanti a me. Ogni volta c'è qualcosa che non torna, la voce si perde. Non so perché ma non è mai abbastanza. Come dici? Forse hai ragione. Più si è feriti e più si è grandi. E più si è vuoti. Mi hanno usato per i loro divertimenti, nutrito di roba scadente. La vita se n'è andata in un momento. È sempre stato così: ho lottato, cercato un orlo, un'alba dove poter ricominciare. Ho passato un'infinità di notti senza dormire. Sono rimasto ore e ore a sudare per distruggere e cadere. Ho fatto di tutto per occupare ogni vuoto. Il sangue brillava nelle mie vene e io, in fondo, ho sempre voluto precipitare.*

*Say that again, please. I can't hear what you're saying. My face is made of bronze, can't you see? Look at my eyes, my ears, this chest. Say it again, if you like. Or save your breath. The words give way before me. Every time there is something that doesn't add up, the voice is lost. I don't know why, but it is never enough. What is that you're saying? Perhaps you're right. The more you're wounded the greater you are. And the more empty you are. They used me for their entertainment, fed on shoddy stuff. Life was over in a moment. It was always like this: I fought, I looked for an edge, a dawn where I could start again. I have endured no end of sleepless nights. I have spent hours and hours sweating to destroy and fall. I did everything to fill up every space. The blood shone in my veins and, basically, I always wanted to drop.*

*Questi che vedi sono i miei guanti sacri alla vita, le mie ferite. Fermati un momento, appoggiaci la mano, guarda. Bisogna succhiare il cuore di un eroe finché batte, lo dovresti sapere. Ho scosso il paese, scrollato le arene, fatto a pezzi gli avversari. Ho illuminato il buio, raccolto gli insulti, costretto agli applausi. Non tutti l'hanno saputo fare. Non te, non voi. D'altronde la vita non è uno spavento per chi non l'ha mai rischiata. Chi mi può capire? Con chi posso ancora parlare? Lo spirito è ammalato, non si può più curare. Sparirà dalla faccia della terra. È il suo destino. Lo so, adesso sono stanco e sto diventando malinconico. È per questo che mi avete scavato la fossa. L'avete aperta lassù, lontano. Per nascondermi. Per non avere problemi e non dover vedere. Stolti! Non potevate immaginare che sarei resuscitato in questo vestito di metallo, che sarei tornato a fissarvi con il mio volto scuro, senza labbra.*

*What you see are my gloves sacred to life, my wounds. Stop a minute, rest your hand there, look. You have to suck the heart of a hero as long as it beats, you ought to know this. I shook the country, made the arenas vibrate, tore my opponents to shreds. I lit up the darkness, collected insults, compelled applause. Not everyone knew how to do this. None of you. On the other hand life is not frightening for those who have never taken a risk. Who can understand me? Who can I still speak to? The spirit is ill, it can no longer be cured. It will disappear off the face of the earth. This is its fate. I know, now I am tired and becoming sad. This is why you have dug me the grave. You have opened it down there, far away. To conceal me. So as not to have problems and not have to see. Fools! You couldn't imagine that I would be resuscitated in this metal suit, that I would come back to stare at you with my dark face, without lips.*

*Tic tac, tic tac…*
*che ognuno mi veda:*

*figura pentita di tutti quei sogni*
*avuti in sorte, presi a pugni,*

*messi da parte.*

*Tick tock, tick tock…*
*let everyone see me:*

*a figure regretting all those dreams*
*I was blessed with, punched,*

*set aside.*

*Tic tac, tic tac…*
*avanzo a piccoli passi,*

*l’ombra si allunga:*
*non c’è grido né stupore*

*—non c’è dolore.*

*Tick tock, tick tock…*
*I proceed in small steps,*

*the shadow lengthens:*
*there's no cry or wonder*

*—there's no pain.*

*Tic tac, tic tac…*
*il pugno cerca la ferita,*

*dà da bere a queste*
*mie avide vene.*

*Tick tock, tick tock…*
*the fist seeks the sore,*

*gives drink to these*
*my thirsty veins.*

*Tic tac, tic tac…*
*vorrei la mia pelle fosse*

*pietra come quell'antica*
*rovina, sgretolarmi a fatica.*

*Tick tock, tick tock...*
*I wish my skin were*

*stone, like that ancient*
*ruin slowly eroding.*

*Tic tac, tic tac…*
*scivolo in un flutto miserabile,*

*schiavo della pena: in quel buio*
*pesto affondo, a caro prezzo rispondo.*

*Tick tock, tick tock…*
*I slip into a miserable flow,*

*slave to pain: in that pitch dark*
*I sink, at a high price respond.*

*Tic tac, tic tac…*
*le urla sono un brivido*

*profondo nella schiena.*

*Tick tock, tick tock…*
*the screams are a deep shiver*

*down my spine.*

*Tic tac, tic tac…*
*abbassa il capo, finta:*

*con quell'occhio fissa il mio*
*paio—spaventa.*

*Tick tock, tick tock…*
*lower your head, feint:*

*with that eye, stare at my*
*pair—it's frightening.*

*Tic tac, tic tac…*
*la ferita lava,*

*la bocca sa di ruggine*
*—di terra, sa di bava.*

*Tick tock, tick tock...*
*the wound washes,*

*the mouth tastes of rust*
*—of earth, of drool.*

*Tic tac, tic tac…*
*all'angolo, al riparo:*

*è casa, tomba*
*—posa?*

*Tick tock, tick tock…*
*in the corner, sheltered:*

*it's home, tomb*
*—pose?*

*Tic tac, tic tac…*
*d’inestinguibile sete*

*ardo.*

*Tick tock, tick tock…*
*with unquenchable thirst*

*I burn.*

*Tic tac, tic tac...*
*non c'è poi molto da scavare*

*in questo conto che è soltanto*
*da saldare.*

*Tick tock, tick tock...*
*there's not much to unearth*

*in this debt that's yet*
*to be paid.*

*Tic tac, tic tac…*
*sono pronto,*

*stringo un patto*
*d'uomo morto.*

*Tick tock, tick tock…*
*I'm ready,*

*I make a dead*
*man's pact.*

*Tic tac, tic tac…*
*datemi ancora due riprese*

*—urli*
*Su le mani,*

*al cuore i guantoni!*

*Tick tock, tick tock…*
*give me two more rounds*

*—you scream*
*Hands up,*

*gloves to the heart!*

*Tic tac, tic tac…*
*cedi sotto colpi*

*troppo duri:*
*braccia in croce,*

*sguardo al cielo.*

*Tick tock, tick tock…*
*you sag beneath blows*

*too hard:*
*arms crossed,*

*eyes to the sky.*

*Tic tac, tic tac…*
*impiccato alle corde*

*soffocato dal peso*
*del corpo—indifeso.*

*Tick tock, tick tock…*
*hung from the ropes*

*smothered by the heft*
*of the body—bereft.*

*Tic tac, tic tac…*
*chiusa la conta*

*costretto a riposo*
*nel bronzo—racconta:*

*Tick tock, tick tock…*
*the count is over*

*forced to rest*
*in bronze—you say:*

*La carne s'è fatta amara, il mio cuore pesta,*
*vorrei riuscire a farlo fuori per una volta.*

*Sono sempre stato uno strano,*
*un buono a nulla, un disgraziato.*

*Non ho mai saputo fare le cose*
*che sapete fare voi, chiacchierare.*

*Ne è passato di tempo e ora grava*
*sul mio capo questa corona*

*colma d'insanabili ferite, di spasmi,*
*di catastrofi. Avete iniziato a seguirmi*

*come fossi un'antica reliquia da venerare.*
*Be' eccomi qui, posato in questo bronzo,*

*logorato dal veleno d'un vecchio inganno,*
*braccato senza tregua da un'oscena vanità.*

*Piangete se credete, piangete sull'impronta*
*di questa conta alla rovescia, di queste vene*

*incendiate da capogiri, da guantoni sgualciti.*
*E il mio sdegno? I miei colpi crudeli?*

*Il mio fiato antico? Sì, tutto questo finirà,*
*non per paura però, non di noia.*

*The flesh has become bitter, my heart pounds.*
*I wish I could do away with it for once.*

*I've always been an oddball,*
*a good-for-nothing, a wretch.*

*I've never been able to do the things*
*that you can do, to chat.*

*Much time has passed and now this crown*
*full of incurable wounds, spasms, catastrophes,*

*weighs heavy on my head.*
*You started to follow me*

*as if I were an ancient relic to worship.*
*Well, here I am, posed in this bronze,*

*worn down by the poison of an old deception,*
*relentlessly hounded by an obscene conceit.*

*Weep if you believe, weep at the marker*
*of this decline, of these veins*

*inflamed by dizziness, by crumpled gloves.*
*And my outrage? My cruel blows?*

*My ancient breath? Yes, all this will end,*
*but not out of fear, not out of boredom.*

*È tutto finito*
*Quante dita son queste?*

*Libero la mente*
*La vedi la mia mano?*

*Riposo la concentrazione*
*Dove ti trovi ora?*

*M'acquieto per un attimo*
*Che round è?*

*Recupero il respiro*
*Finiscilo!*

*Urla forte il gorgo profondo*
*Finiscilo!*

*Si sgola la cavea furiosa*
*Finiscilo!*

*Sento abbaiarmi addosso.*
*Mi fermo a guardarlo.*

*È di nuovo in piedi.*
*Non chiede compassione.*

*Soltanto cerca un po' di verità,*
*una nuova ferita.*

*It's all over*
*How many fingers do you see?*

*I free my mind*
*Can you see my hand?*

*I rest my concentration*
*Where are you now?*

*I calm myself for a moment*
*What round is it?*

*I get back my breath*
*End it!*

*The deep vortex shouts loudly*
*End it!*

*The furious audience shouts itself hoarse*
*End it!*

*I hear him barking at me.*
*I stop to look at him.*

*He is on his feet again.*
*He asks for no mercy.*

*He seeks only a little truth,*
*a new wound.*

*…*
*va tutto*
*bene*
*mi sento*
*bene*
*colpisco*
*bene*
*preciso*
*duro*

*ci siamo!*
*supero*
*il limite*
*non sento*
*più nulla*
*ora*
*vedo però*
*la sua smorfia*
*è una smorfia*
*di dolore*
*capisco che*
*sta soffrendo*
*che sente*
*come un blocco*
*una morsa*
*pare prigioniero*
*del suo stesso corpo*
*si sbilancia*
*pare cedere*
*no!*
*è ancora lì*
*ha quell'occhio*
*quell'occhio fisso*
*con quello*

*m'incalza*
*mi tampina*
*avanza*
*torno*
*a sentire*
*ora*
*delle voci*
*urlano*
*sento*
*chiamare forte*
*il mio nome*
*ecco!*
*ci siamo!*
*non sento*
*più nulla*
*supero*
*il limite*
*colpisco*
*veloce*
*danzo*
*leggero*
*va tutto*
*bene*
*mi sento*
*bene*
*colpisco*
*e mi muovo*
*bene*
*a brevi falcate*
*a piccoli passi*
*giro*
*dove devo*
*faccio tutto*
*come si deve*

*lui si fa sotto*
*mi colpisce*
*fa caldo*
*sento*
*il mio corpo*
*libero*
*sento*
*ogni fibra in me*
*che reagisce*
*continuo a muovermi*
*e a colpire*

*ci siamo!*
*lui accusa*
*i miei colpi*
*capisco che*
*devo tener duro*
*e andare avanti*
*mi colpisce*
*in faccia*
*esonda in me*
*dolore puro*
*inarginato*
*mi tocco*
*la piaga*
*è aperta*
*esonda sangue*
*ma non è*
*niente*
*va tutto*
*bene*
*è solo*
*sangue*
*lo fisso*

*quell'occhio*
*ricambia*
*ma sto*
*bene*

*ci siamo!*
*non vedo*
*più nulla*
*sento*
*sento soltanto*
*un gran calore*
*venire su*
*e il mio corpo*
*rantolare*
*sboccare*
*è il mio corpo*
*sì*
*il mio corpo*
*che rantola*
*schiuma*
*avvampa*
*sono tutte*
*fitte*
*quelle che sento*
*è tutto*
*dolore*
*quello che provo*
*ma dura*
*un attimo*
*dura*
*un attimo*
*soltanto*
*è tutto finito*
*è andato*

*come doveva*
*come avrei voluto*
*non andasse*
*mi guardo*
*come da lontano*
*la piaga aperta*
*sbotta ancora*
*sangue*
*ma va bene*
*così*
*ho sempre vissuto*
*così*
*in un mare*
*rosso*
*rosso*
*di sangue*
*mi guardo*
*e mi vedo*
*una lontananza*
*e tutto*
*è splendore*
*lì dove sono*
*tutto*
*è calma*
*e voluttà*
*e piacere*
*tutto*
*è amore*
*mi guardo*
*e vedo un uomo*
*un uomo soltanto.*

*...*
*everything's*
*good*
*I feel*
*good*
*I hit*
*good*
*right on*
*hard*

*we're there!*
*I cross*
*the limit*
*I no longer feel*
*anything*
*but I see*
*his grimace*
*it's a grimace*
*of pain*
*I realize that*
*he's hurting*
*that he feels*
*like a block*
*a grip*
*he seems*
*a prisoner*
*of his own body*
*he sways*
*seems*
*to give way*
*no!*
*he's still there*
*he has that stare*
*that fixed stare*

*with it*
*he crowds me*
*shadows me*
*advances*
*I can again hear*
*voices now*
*shouting*
*I hear*
*my name*
*called loudly*
*here!*
*we are!*
*I no longer feel*
*anything*
*I cross*
*the limit*
*I strike*
*fast*
*dance*
*light*
*everything's*
*good*
*I feel*
*good*
*I hit and move*
*good*
*in short skips*
*small steps*
*I turn*
*where I have to*
*do everything*
*as I should*
*he gets under*
*he hits me*

*it's hot*
*I feel*
*my body*
*free*
*I feel*
*every fiber in me*
*that reacts*
*I keep moving*
*and hitting*

*we're there!*
*he's feeling*
*my blows*
*I know I have to*
*hold fast*
*and carry on*
*he hits me*
*in the face*
*a rush*
*goes through me pure*
*unstemmed*
*pain*
*I touch myself*
*the wound*
*is open*
*it spurts blood*
*but it's*
*nothing*
*everything's*
*good*
*it's only*
*blood*
*I stare at him*
*he stares*

*back*
*but I'm*
*good*

*we're there!*
*I see*
*nothing now*
*I feel*
*I only feel*
*a great heat*
*rising*
*and my body*
*gasp*
*gush*
*it's my body*
*yes*
*my body*
*that gasps*
*foams*
*burns*
*all I can*
*sense*
*is spasm*
*all I can*
*feel*
*is pain*
*but it lasts*
*a moment*
*it lasts*
*only*
*a moment*
*it's all over*
*it went*
*as it had to*

*as I would*
*have wanted*
*it not to*
*I look at myself*
*as if from a distance*
*the open wound*
*still spurting*
*blood*
*but it's ok*
*like this*
*I've always lived*
*like this*
*in a red*
*red*
*sea*
*of blood*
*I look at myself*
*and see myself*
*a distance*
*and everything*
*is splendor*
*in the place I am*
*everything*
*is calm*
*and rapture*
*and pleasure*
*everything*
*is love*
*I look at myself*
*and see a man*
*just a man.*

ERIS

265 Riverside Drive
New York 10025



ISBN 978-1-971559-07-0

Gabriele Tinti is an Italian poet whose work engages with classical sculpture and museum collections. His writing has been presented in collaboration with institutions including the J. Paul Getty Museum, the Metropolitan Museum of Art, the British Museum, the Los Angeles County Museum of Art, the Museo Nazionale Romano, and the Glyptothek of Munich. His recent books include *Ruins*, *Bleedings*, *Confessions*, and *Hungry Ghosts*.

David Graham is a translator working from Italian into English. He translates catalogues for art exhibitions and museums, including the Venice Biennale and the Accademia di Belle Arti di Venezia, and also works with poetry. He grew up in New Zealand and moved to Europe in 1982. He lives in Venice.

Nicholas Benson is a translator working from Italian into English. His translations include Attilio Bertolucci's *Winter Journey*; Aldo Palazzeschi's *The Arsonist*, for which he received an NEA Translation Fellowship; and, with Elena Coda, Scipio Slataper's *My Karst and My City*, which received the 2022 John Florio Prize from the Society of Authors (UK).